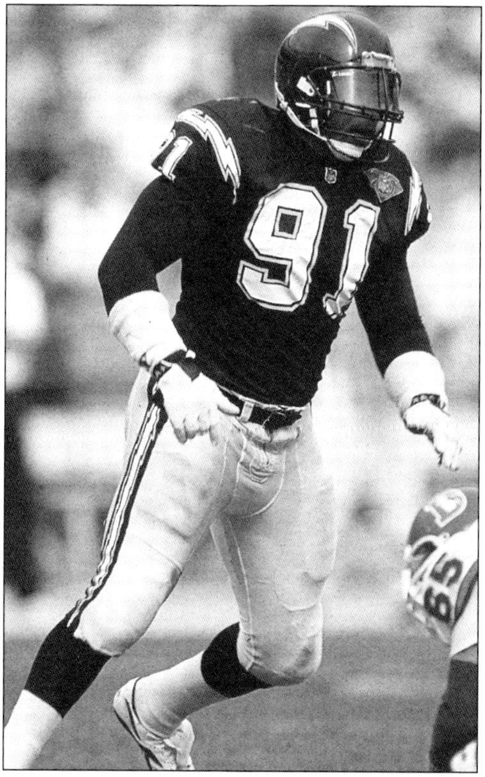

CREATIVE EDUCATION

SAN DIEGO CHARGERS

JULIE NELSON

Published by Creative Education
123 South Broad Street, Mankato, Minnesota 56001
Creative Education is an imprint of The Creative Company

Designed by Rita Marshall

Photos by: Active Images, Allsport USA, AP/Wide World Photos,
Bettmann/CORBIS, SportsChrome

Copyright © 2001 Creative Education.
International copyrights reserved in all countries.
No part of this book may be reproduced in any form without written
permission from the publisher.
Printed in the United States of America.

Library of Congress Cataloging-in-Publication Data

Nelson, Julie.
San Diego Chargers / by Julie Nelson.
p. cm. — (NFL today)
Summary: Traces the history of the team from its beginnings through 1999.
ISBN 1-58341-058-9

1. San Diego Chargers (Football team)—History—Juvenile literature. [1. San
Diego Chargers (Football team)—History. 2. Football—History.] I. Title.
II. Series: NFL today (Mankato, Minn.)

GV956.S29N45   2000
796.332'64'09794985—dc21   99-015757

First edition

9 8 7 6 5 4 3 2 1

Forty years ago, the city of San Diego, California, had fewer than 350,000 residents. Today, more than 1.1 million people call San Diego home. There are many reasons for this population explosion: the city's sunny yet mild climate, its business as a major port city, and such attractions as the world-famous San Diego Zoo.

Excitement and fun—that's San Diego. It's also a good description of the city's professional football team, the Chargers. For more than 40 years, the San Diego Chargers have entertained fans with high-powered offenses highlighted by some of the league's most explosive passing attacks.

Hall of Fame receiver Lance Alworth.

Halfback Paul Lowe led San Diego's offense with 855 rushing yards.

San Diego's first coach, Sid Gillman, had built a National Football League championship team with the Los Angeles Rams by relying on the pass. In 1959, Gillman and the Rams parted company, and Gillman joined the Los Angeles Chargers, a first-year team in the new American Football League.

Gillman signed the team's first two offensive stars: halfback Paul Lowe and quarterback Jack Kemp. Behind Lowe and Kemp, the Chargers won the 1960 AFL Western Division with a 10–4 record before falling to the Houston Oilers in the league title game. But despite this success, the Chargers didn't win many Los Angeles fans. The Rams were top dogs in Los Angeles, so Chargers owner Barron Hilton decided to move his team down the California coast to San Diego.

Gillman then set out to gather some stars. He managed to sign such great college players as running back Keith Lincoln and defensive linemen Earl Faison and Ernie Ladd. These new standouts teamed with holdovers Kemp, Lowe, and powerful offensive lineman Ron Mix to lead the first-year San Diego Chargers to the Western Division title in 1961 with a 12–2 record. But, for the second straight year, the Chargers fell to Houston in the AFL championship game.

THE ALWORTH AND HADL ATTACK

Before the start of the 1962 season, the Chargers traded for Lance Alworth, a shifty wide receiver with speed, jumping ability, and the coordination of a gymnast. Alworth was injured during much of the 1962 season. In fact, more than half of the team's players were injured that year, and the Chargers slumped to a 4–10 record.

A defensive leader, safety Rodney Harrison.

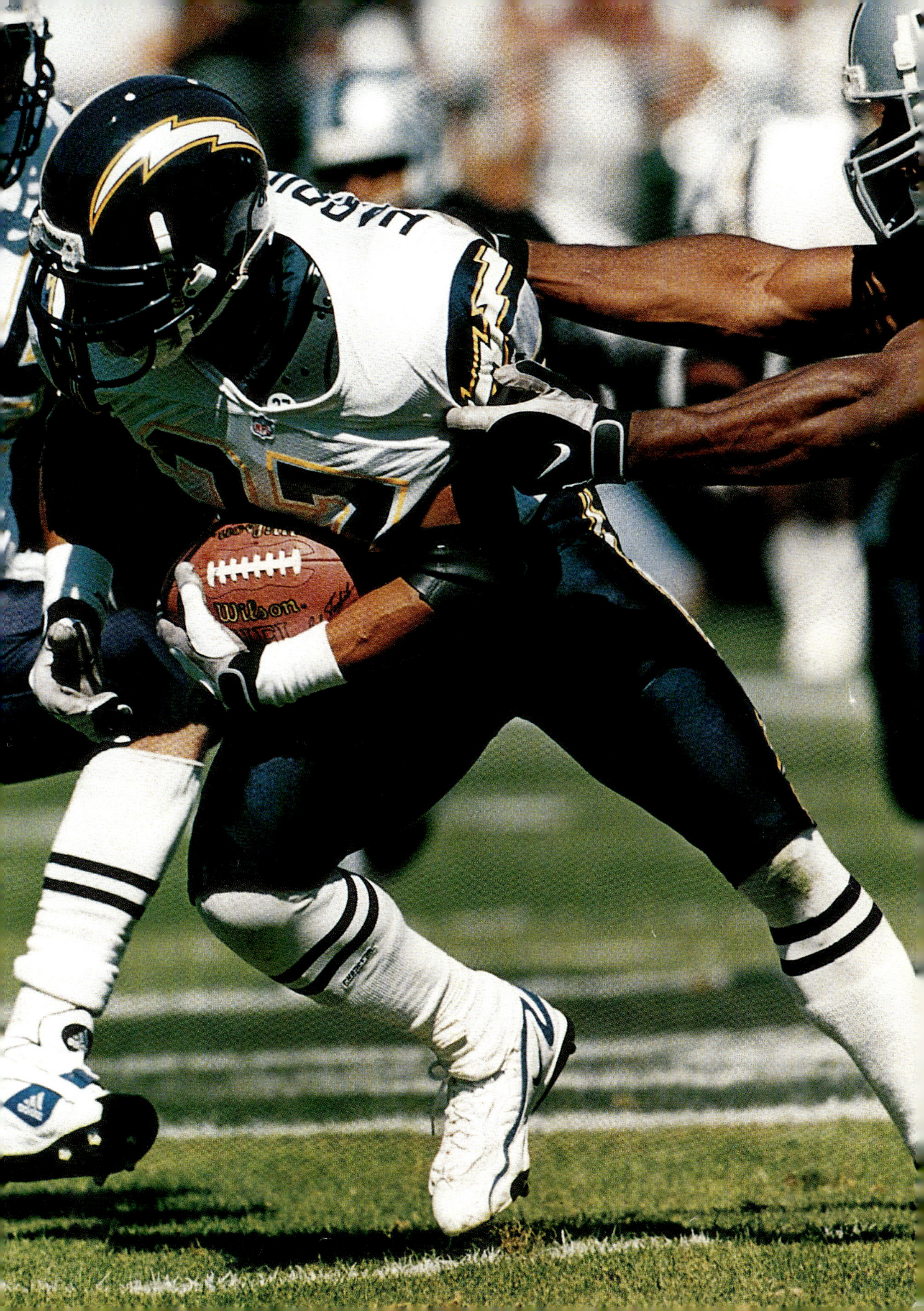
Wilson

1963

Quarterback Tobin Rote completed nearly 60 percent of his passes.

The following year, Lowe and Alworth were healthy again, and Gillman brought in a new quarterback—veteran Tobin Rote—to replace Jack Kemp. Rote led the AFL in passing in 1963 with 2,510 yards and 20 touchdowns, while Alworth caught at least one touchdown pass in each of nine straight games.

Alworth's energetic running style, which resembled that of a deer, earned him a unique nickname: "Bambi." "I used to love to watch him line up and take his stance," said Al Locasale, one of the founders of the Chargers franchise. "His free hand shaking, all the adrenaline pumping, all that energy ready to explode."

The Chargers' offense averaged more than 28 points per game as the team moved into first place in the Western Division. Late in the season, Rote developed arm trouble, so Gillman handed the reins to John Hadl. The young quarterback threw five touchdown passes in a 47–23 victory over Denver that clinched the division title.

The underdog Chargers then traveled to Boston for the AFL championship game against the Boston Patriots. San Diego racked up three touchdowns in the first quarter and won 51–10 in a blowout. Keith Lincoln rushed for 206 yards, and Hadl and Rote combined for 285 passing yards.

After winning its first championship, San Diego captured Western Division titles in 1964 and 1965 but lost both years to the Buffalo Bills in the league championship game. The key player for the Chargers was John Hadl, who took over as starting quarterback in 1964 and never looked back.

Hadl specialized in leading late-game drives to pull out last-second victories. "I call him 'Cliff-hanger Hadl,'" Gillman said.

"If the game goes down to the final minute, John is the best guy in the league at pulling something out of the hat." In 1965, Hadl led the AFL in passing with 2,798 yards and 20 touchdowns. Many of those touchdown passes went to the speedy Alworth, who had the best year of his remarkable career with 1,602 yards receiving—a team record that still stands.

Unfortunately for Hadl and Alworth, their heroics couldn't produce another division championship. Defensive stars Ernie Ladd and Earl Faison were no longer with the team, and the depleted defense gave up more than 20 points per game in 1966. The Chargers slumped to third place in the division with a 7–6–1 record.

San Diego had lost its championship luster. From 1967 through 1969, the high-scoring Chargers managed winning records every year but finished behind the Oakland Raiders and Kansas City Chiefs. Even though the team couldn't rise to the top, Alworth and Hadl stayed there. Alworth led the league in receiving yardage in 1968 and 1969, and Hadl was consistently among the AFL leaders in passing yardage.

In 1970, the AFL and NFL merged into one league, and the Chargers were placed in the Western Division of the American Football Conference. In 10 seasons in the AFL, San Diego had won one league title and five division championships. But the team had gotten old, and Gillman had stepped down as coach.

After a series of unsuccessful coaches, new owner Eugene Klein hired Tommy Prothro midway through 1973. The team also had a new quarterback. In the 1973 NFL draft, the Chargers acquired Dan Fouts, a star passer out of the University of Oregon. As Fouts sat on the bench for his first few

Towering defensive tackle Ernie Ladd was named to the All-AFL team.

Intelligent quarterback Stan Humphries.

Sure-handed halfback Ronnie Harmon.

Receiver Lance Alworth played his final season with the Chargers.

years, the Chargers finished last in the AFC Western Division in 1973, 1974, and 1975.

In 1976, Prothro decided it was time to make Fouts the permanent starter. To provide Fouts with a talented passing target, Prothro used the Chargers' top pick in the 1978 draft to take Arizona State wide receiver John Jefferson. Prothro also brought in another receiver, Charlie Joiner, through a trade with the Cincinnati Bengals.

The team had the ingredients for a great offense, but Prothro wouldn't be around to see the final result. After the Chargers opened the 1978 season with a victory over the Seattle Seahawks, the team lost three games in a row. Prothro resigned, and Don Coryell became the new head coach. Coryell loved the pass, and he wasn't afraid to use it at any time.

Fouts Becomes Pilot of "Air Coryell"

After a loss to the New England Patriots, the Chargers rebounded to defeat Denver 23–0. It would prove to be the game that turned San Diego's fortunes around. Led by Dan Fouts, the team won 19 of its next 26 games during the 1978 and 1979 seasons.

"We're only doing what we do because of Dan," Coach Coryell said. "He has such a flexible mind. He doesn't have all the qualities you'd want in an ideal quarterback. He's not a runner. He's a fine athlete, but he doesn't have the speed. But he is very, very intelligent, and he is extremely competitive and tough mentally."

In 1979, Fouts broke the NFL single-season passing yardage record, throwing for 4,082 yards. He also tossed 24 touchdown passes to lead the Chargers to a 12–4 record that year, good enough to win the AFC Western Division title. Running back Chuck Muncie gave San Diego an effective ground game to complement a passing attack that everyone was calling "Air Coryell."

"We're going to throw the ball," Fouts said, "and we don't care who knows it." In San Diego's first playoff game, however, the Houston Oilers managed to shut down Air Coryell, beating the Chargers 17–14.

The following season, Air Coryell started moving at supersonic speed. Fouts led the team to an 11–5 record, good for another division title. After a first-round playoff victory over Buffalo, though, the Chargers came up short against the Oakland Raiders in the AFC title game.

1 9 8 0

Tight end Kellen Winslow had a career year, catching 89 passes.

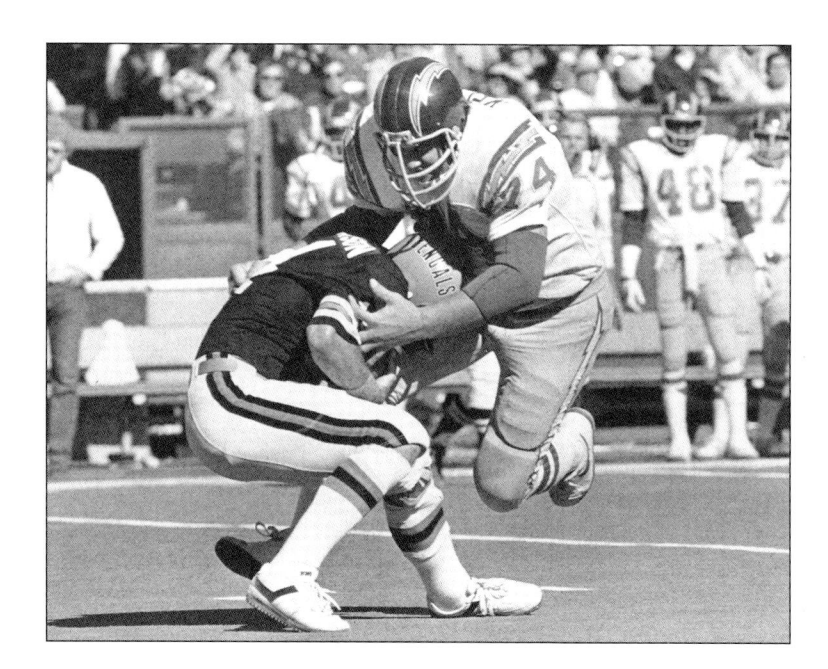

Tough defensive tackle Louie Kelcher.

1 9 8 1

Head coach Don Coryell and his "Air Coryell" offense led San Diego to a 10–6 record.

Air Coryell was grounded, but only temporarily. The Chargers won the division title again in 1981—the team's third straight. Everyone knew about Fouts and the high-powered offense, but the San Diego defense could be just as dangerous. Defensive linemen Louie Kelcher, Fred Dean, and Gary "Big Hands" Johnson were capable of dominating the line of scrimmage.

In the first round of the playoffs, though, the defense had a rough time as Miami took a 38–31 advantage into the fourth quarter. Fouts then tossed a late touchdown pass to tie the game and send it into overtime. Finally, San Diego's Rolf Benirschke kicked the game-winning field goal to give the Chargers a thrilling 41–38 victory.

A week later, in frigid Cincinnati, San Diego lost its second consecutive AFC title game, 27–7, to the Bengals. "I can't tell you how much it hurts to come this far and lose two years in a row," said a dejected Coach Coryell.

JOINER LEADS THE CHARGE

The Chargers wouldn't have a chance to play in a third straight AFC title game in 1982. The team made the playoffs but lost to Miami in the second round. The next three seasons were a series of turns for the worse. Defensive mainstays Dean, Kelcher, and Johnson all left San Diego, and tight end Kellen Winslow suffered a horrible knee injury. Fouts and wide receiver Wes Chandler, who replaced the traded John Jefferson, were plagued by a series of ailments. Through all this adversity, however, there was one constant—receiver Charlie Joiner.

San Diego's all-time sacks leader, Leslie O'Neal.

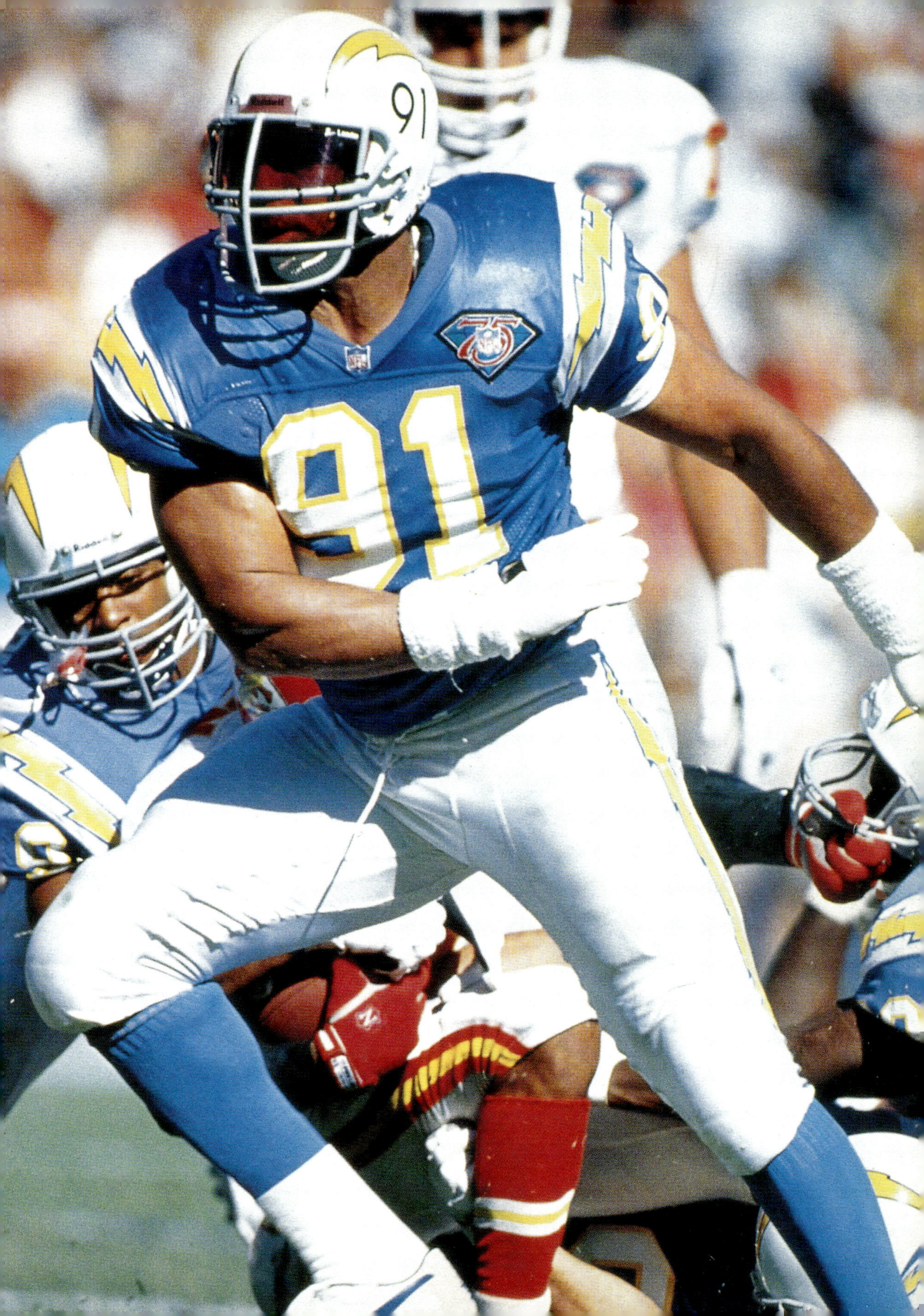
91

Charlie Joiner was a brilliant route runner.

"I don't recall him ever missing a practice at all since I've been in San Diego," Coryell said. "One time, he cracked a rib and didn't take one day off. He said, 'I'll work through it.'" Assistant coach Ernie Zampese agreed: "He honest-to-God believes that if you miss one practice, you'll lose something."

Joiner, rather small at 5-foot-11 and 185 pounds, had some speed, but his biggest asset on the field was his mind. Coaching legend Bill Walsh once called Joiner "the most intelligent receiver the game has ever known."

Joiner became the Chargers' "go-to" man when regular pass patterns broke down and Fouts was pressured in the pocket. "When I'm back there in the pocket," Fouts explained, "I can tell when Charlie's going to be open, and at the last minute, I'll look to a spot and there he'll be. And he'll catch the ball."

Joiner's precise pass routes and understanding of defensive coverages helped open up opportunities for San Diego's other receivers as well. After one game in 1984, a newspaper reporter asked Kellen Winslow how he was able to get open to catch 10 passes that day. Winslow pointed toward Joiner's locker and said, "Ask him."

In 1984, Joiner became the all-time leading pass receiver in NFL history, surpassing former Washington Redskins star Charley Taylor. When Joiner retired after the 1986 season, he had caught 750 passes for 12,146 yards—both NFL records.

Joiner's last season was also the Chargers' worst season since 1975. San Diego finished 4–12 in 1986. The days of Air Coryell were over. New coach Al Saunders had tried instead to build the team around a strong defense. In spite of the Chargers' failures in 1986, two young defensive linemen had

Wes Chandler set a new Chargers record with 260 receiving yards in a single game.

Unlike Joiner, Natrone Means relied on raw power (pages 18-19).

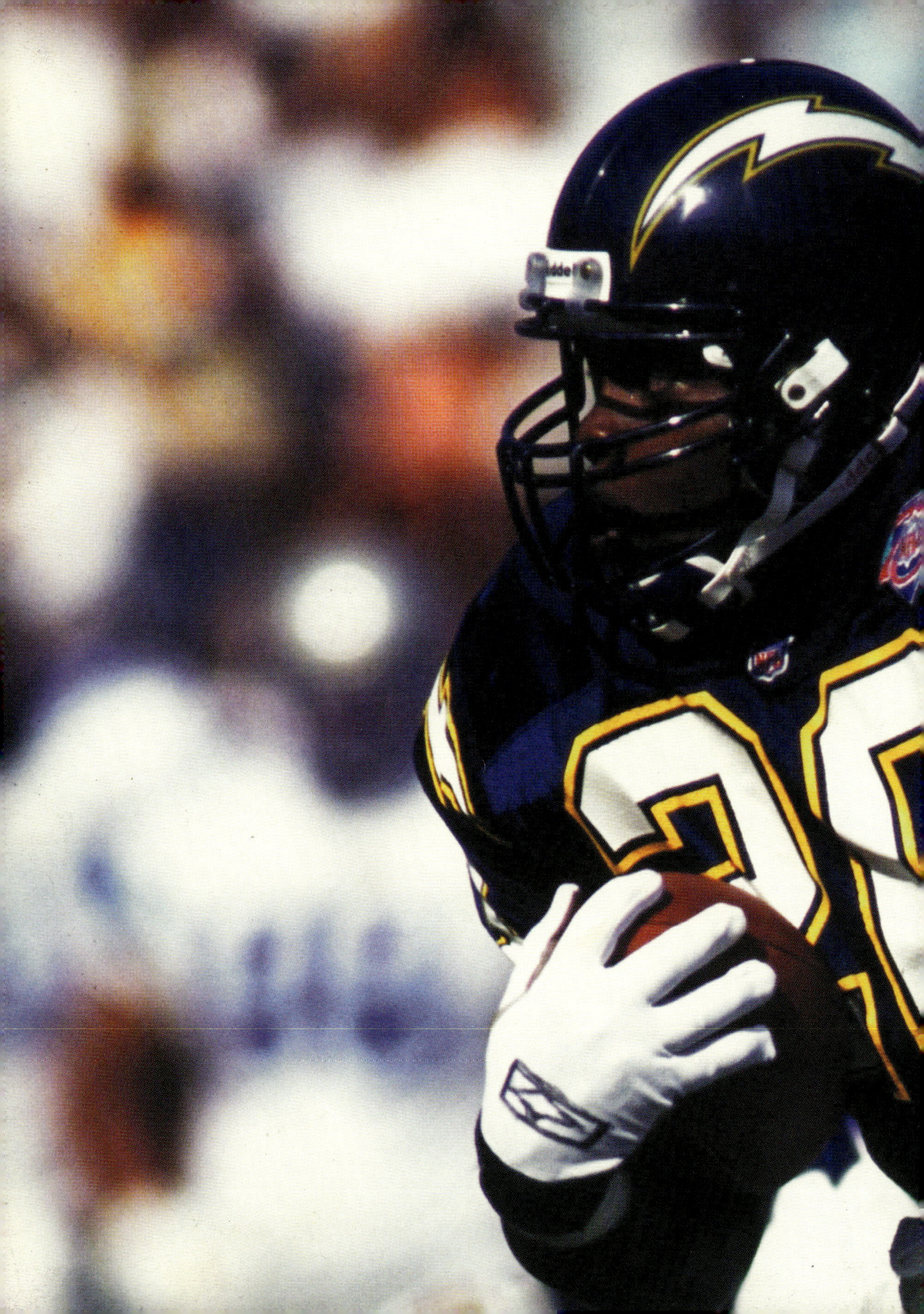

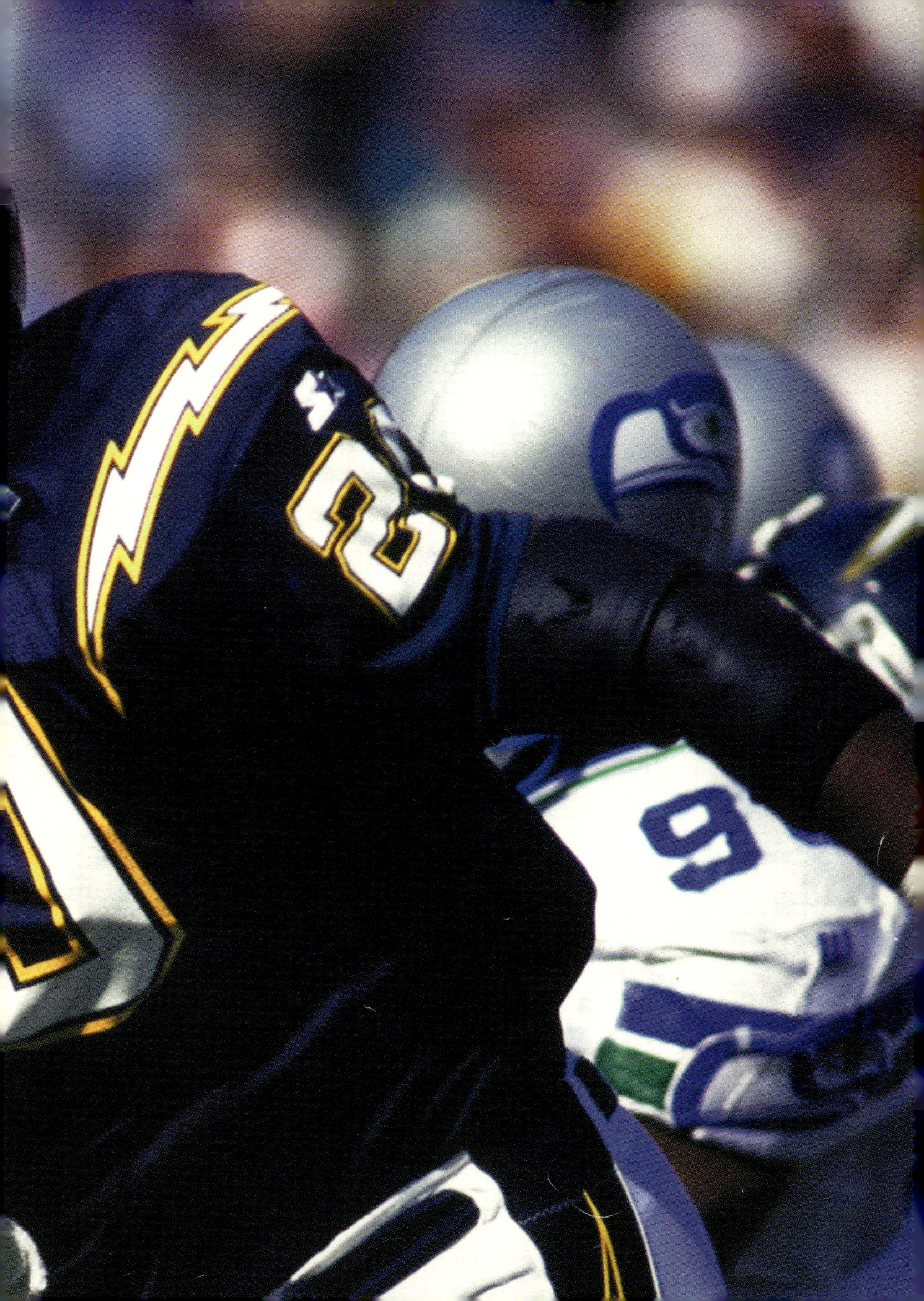

Cornerback Gill Byrd led all defenders with seven interceptions.

great years for San Diego. Lee Williams registered 15 quarterback sacks, the second most in the AFC, while Leslie O'Neal had 12.5 sacks.

The improved defense and a healthy Dan Fouts keyed an 8–1 start in 1987. O'Neal was injured, but Williams, linebacker Billy Ray Smith, and cornerback Gill Byrd led the stingy San Diego defense. The Chargers rose to the dizzying heights of first place in the AFC Western Division but lost their last six games and wound up third in the division. It was the beginning of the end for Saunders, who was fired after a 6–10 season in 1988.

After the 1989 season, the Chargers found a man who would be the architect of San Diego's revival. Bobby Beathard had been responsible for rebuilding the Washington Redskins a decade earlier, and some experts called him the smartest man in football. Beathard became San Diego's new general manager, responsible for finding the players and coaches to make the team a winner again.

A New Era

In the 1990 NFL draft, Beathard proved once again that he was a superb judge of football talent. He made linebacker Junior Seau, out of the University of Southern California, the Chargers' number one pick that year. Seau would go on to become the heart of the San Diego defense and one of the greatest linebackers in league history.

Seau was an instant terror in the NFL—an intelligent player who could bench-press 500 pounds and run like a receiver. Bill Belichick, head coach of the Cleveland Browns, was amazed. "Junior Seau is the best defensive player we've faced, I'd say, by a pretty good margin," he said. "He does it all. He can play at the point of attack, he chases down plays, he plays the run, he plays the pass. He's a guy nobody's really been able to stop."

Seau's contributions went beyond the playing field as well. He devoted himself to numerous charitable causes in the San Diego area, including the establishment of the Junior Seau Foundation to combat child abuse and delinquency and to steer kids away from alcohol and drugs.

Seau was inspired by his own childhood experiences to help others. As a boy, he overcame the challenges of a new culture when he moved with his family from American Samoa to Oceanside, California. Seau did not learn to speak

Defensive end Leslie O'Neal tore into opposing backfields for 13.5 sacks.

Defensive end Lee Williams.

Phenomenal passer Dan Fouts.

English until age seven, yet he went on to make the California high school All-Academic football team with a 3.6 grade-point average. "When I was growing up," Seau explained, "my family didn't have a lot of money, but we did have a lot of love, and I had my dreams. The Junior Seau Foundation was created to help empower and educate young people so they can achieve their dreams. I hope young people see that dreams really do come true."

Seau provided strength and character to the Chargers, but there were two more crucial pieces to the rebuilding puzzle, and Beathard acquired them both in 1992. The first was a new head coach. Beathard's choice was Bobby Ross, who had led the Georgia Tech football team to a national college championship in 1990.

"He's a tough, demanding coach, but at the same time, a fair guy," Beathard said of Ross. "He's not going to ask players to do anything he wouldn't do himself. People seem to respond to his coaching. He's going to win by getting absolutely the most out of his players."

The second key addition to the Chargers was quarterback Stan Humphries. He had been a backup in Washington while Beathard was general manager there, and Beathard was convinced that Humphries had gained enough experience to assume starting duties in San Diego. Humphries proved him right, winning the respect of his Chargers teammates with his leadership abilities and physical toughness. On numerous occasions, Humphries played through injuries that might have kept other quarterbacks on the bench.

In 1992, Ross and his field general Humphries led San Diego to an 11–5 record, the AFC Western Division title, and

1 9 9 2

Under new coach Bobby Ross, the Chargers roared to 11 wins in their last 12 games.

Powerful running back Marion Butts led San Diego with 746 rushing yards.

its first playoff appearance in 10 years. The Chargers upended the Kansas City Chiefs 17–0 in the opening round before falling to the Miami Dolphins.

But all that was a mere prelude to the remarkable 1994 season. Sparked by star running back Natrone Means, San Diego again won the AFC Western Division. Means set an all-time club record with 1,350 rushing yards, while Humphries threw for 3,209 passing yards to give the Chargers a well-balanced attack. In the playoffs, San Diego edged Miami 22–21 in the first round. Then, in a dramatic upset, the Chargers defeated the Pittsburgh Steelers 17–13 on the Steelers' home field to earn the AFC championship. Junior Seau led the defense with an incredible 16 tackles. San Diego was on its way to its first-ever Super Bowl.

Dangerous receiver Anthony Miller.

Unfortunately, the Chargers could not keep up with the San Francisco 49ers—who scored touchdowns on four of their first five possessions—and lost Super Bowl XXIX by a lopsided 49–26 margin. The Chargers returned to the playoffs again in 1995 after winning their last five games to finish 9–7. In the first round of the playoffs, however, San Diego fell 35–20 to Indianapolis in the AFC Wild Card game.

SEARCHING FOR A SPARK

Stan Humphries continued to serve as Chargers field general for the next two seasons. In 1997, however, his willingness to play through injuries caught up with him. A series of concussions kept him on the bench for the final seven starts of the year and led to his retirement at the end of the season.

Under Humphries, the Chargers had finished 8–8 in 1996 and were 4–5 at the time of his last start in 1997. But with its leader out of action, San Diego failed to win another game in 1997, finishing the year with a 4–12 record.

It was obvious that the Chargers needed a new quarterback, and in 1998, they took drastic measures to acquire one. Trading away two veteran players and what amounted to two seasons' worth of draft choices, San Diego dealt with Arizona for the right to the second overall pick in the 1998 NFL draft. With it, the Chargers selected Ryan Leaf, a 6-foot-5 quarterback with a strong arm and unlimited potential.

Although he had earned Heisman Trophy consideration and a lot of media attention with his outstanding play at Washington State, Leaf was smart enough to know that he

1995

Receiver Tony Martin caught 90 passes for a total of 1,224 yards.

The Chargers are known for their aggressive defense (page 26-27).

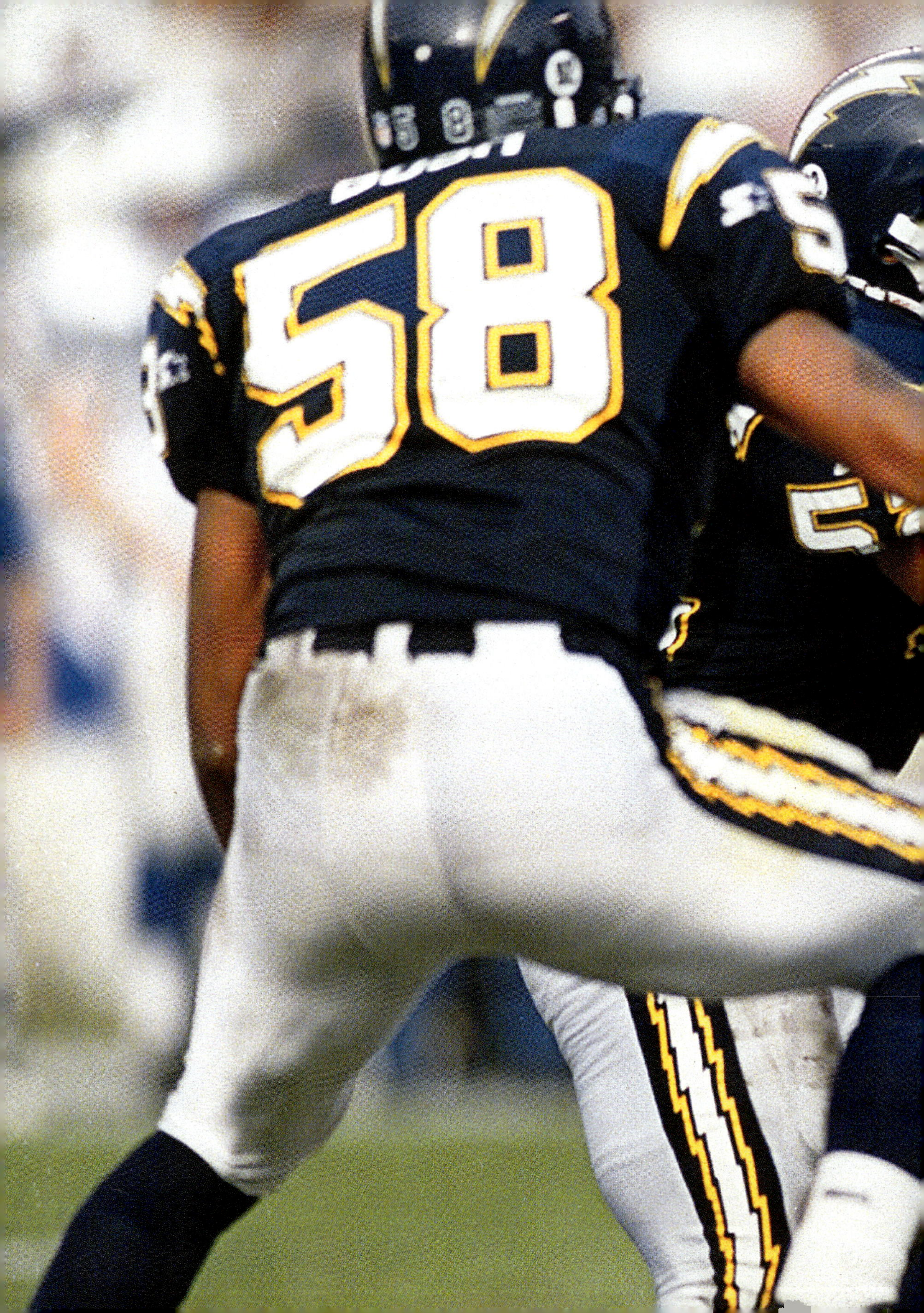
58

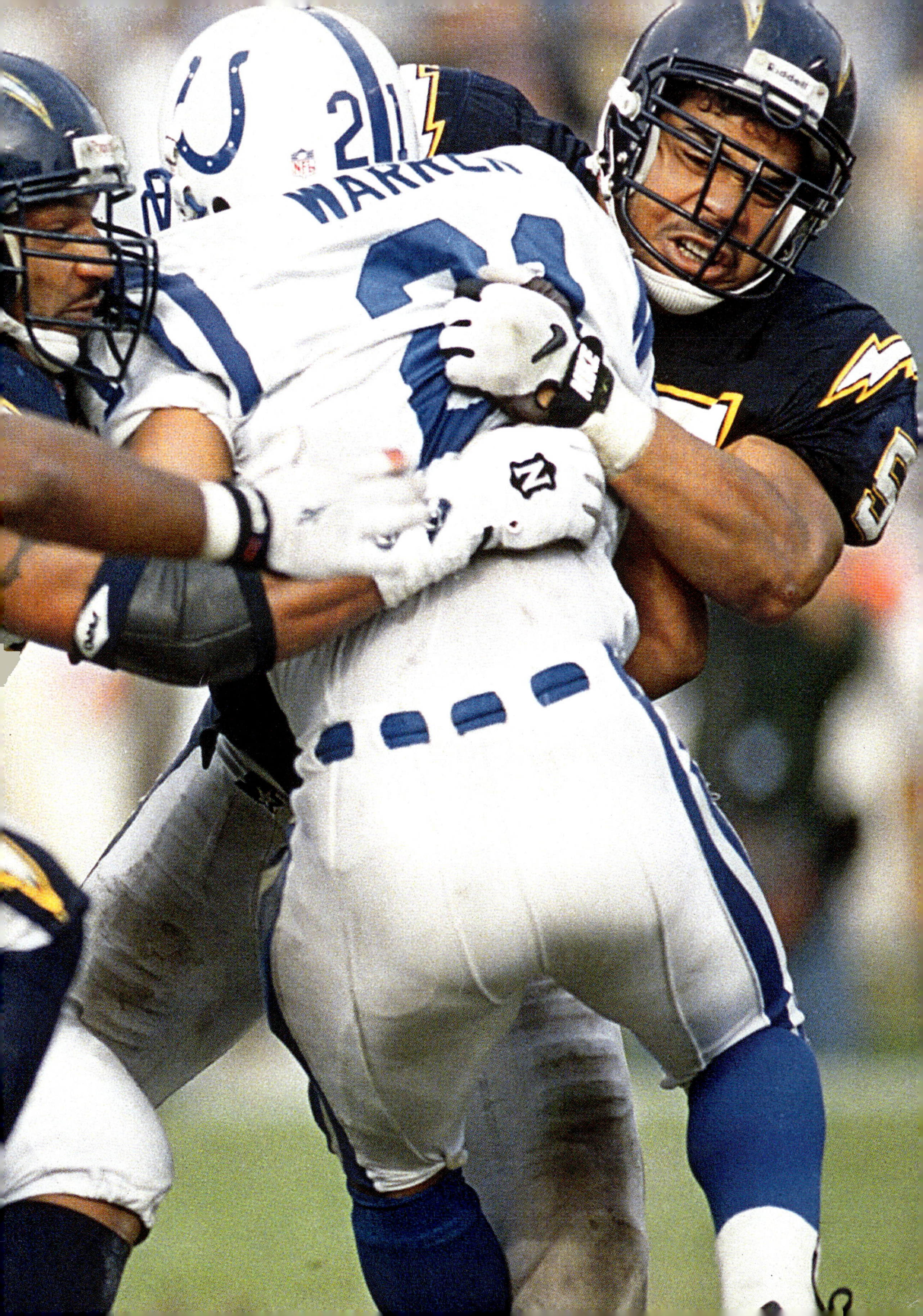

Jeff Graham had a breakthrough season with 968 receiving yards.

needed to improve to play at the NFL level. "I'm not polished," he admitted. "But I can improve every time I step on the field. The great coaches in the NFL can turn me into a great quarterback."

Leaf's youth and inexperience were evident from the start of his rookie season. After nine games in 1998, Leaf had the lowest quarterback rating in the league, having thrown 13 interceptions and only two touchdowns. His behavior off the field was suspect as well, as the hot-tempered quarterback delivered well-publicized outbursts at reporters and teammates alike. June Jones, who had taken over as head coach during the season, benched Leaf in midseason.

Backup Craig Whelihan was given the call to quarterback, but the season could not be salvaged. The Chargers finished

Strong-armed quarterback Ryan Leaf.

5–11, losing their last five games in the process. Although San Diego boasted the NFL's top-ranked defense—led by Seau, safeties Rodney Harrison and Greg Jackson, and defensive end Raylee Johnson—no amount of defense could make up for the Chargers' anemic offense, which committed a league-leading 51 turnovers in 1998.

The offense had problems at other positions besides quarterback. Tony Martin, who had led the Chargers in receiving yards for three straight years, was traded prior to the season, and no other wide receiver was able to step up and fill the void. Running back Natrone Means returned to San Diego in 1998 after two seasons in Jacksonville, but his productivity was hampered by a broken foot.

After the off-season retirement of June Jones, the Chargers hired Mike Riley as their new head coach. Riley, formerly the head man at Oregon State, was just the kind of offense-oriented coach the team needed to work with Leaf. "We've got to teach him what being a pro is all about," Riley said of his young quarterback. "He's part of the big picture, the key to our future."

The Chargers also brought in 13-year veteran quarterback Jim Harbaugh. "Captain Comeback," as Harbaugh was known for his playmaking abilities late in games, was just the sort of example the Chargers wanted for Leaf. Unfortunately, Leaf would have to wait to learn under the veteran, as shoulder surgery sidelined him for the 1999 season.

Injuries and inconsistent quarterback play limited the effectiveness of the Chargers offense in 1999. With Means bothered by knee problems, the Chargers' running game was one of the NFL's worst. Despite the team's offensive

Receiver Curtis Conway emerged as a key weapon on offense.

"Captain Comeback," quarterback Jim Harbaugh.

The anchor of the Chargers defense, Junior Seau.

woes, San Diego's defense—led by Seau and powerful pass rusher Raylee Johnson—once again kept the Chargers competitive. Receiver Jeff Graham was another bright spot, emerging as a much-needed deep threat. Although the Chargers played well at the beginning and end of the season, they finished a mere 8–8.

The Chargers have electrified fans in southern California for more than 40 years. And as the city of San Diego has grown, so have the Chargers' goals. Now, with Seau and receiver Curtis Conway leading the way, today's team hopes to again contend for its first NFL championship.